AF873720

PRODUCTIVITY MEASUREMENT: SOME THEORETICAL UNDERPINNINGS

by

Zenon S. Zannetos
William B. Lindsley
Themis A. Papageorgiou
Ming-Je Tang

December 1981 1251-81

This research has been supported by the U.S. Department of Transportation Contract #DTRS 5681-C-00021.

TABLE OF CONTENTS

I. INTRODUCTION

In the past decade the U.S. industrial power has shown some signs of weakening -- both in absolute and relative terms. This realization has elicited a good deal of concern on the part of both the business and government sectors and has encouraged a considerable amount of research into the subject.

One of the major purported reasons for this deterioration of industrial power is believed to be the decline in U.S. productivity, especially in such major manufacturing industries as automobiles, steel, and shipbuilding.

Many experts, and even more non-experts, have given opinions on the causes underlying the decline of past productivity and on remedies for the future. We present in Table 1 a collection of such ideas from Peat, Marwick, Mitchell & Co., 1981[1]. The set of professionals who support these ideas is impressive, but the disarray of conclusions and recommendations leads us to observe that the productivity problem is indeed very complex, and that the esoteric nature of this issue and the obvious disagreement of experts offer numerous opportunities for new strategic, economic, and policy research. It is to this opportunity for research that we have addressed ourselves.

With a great deal of excellent research has been conducted as regards productivity, much of the work does not provide meaningful information to those who might be in a position to remedy the situation through strategy and policy at the point of resource allocation. It is for this reason that in this study we focus on productivity at the industry and firm level rather that of the economy as a whole. If successful, this attempt will place the resulting data in an associative context which can provide meaning for decision-makers. Thus, it will generate information (signals) motivating

---

[1]As the reader who will consult this volume (Peat, Marwick, Mitchell) will observe these "opinions" are distilled from statements made by these experts

	CAUSES OF PRODUCTIVITY DECLINE IN RECENT YEARS	REMEDIES FOR INCREASED FUTURE PRODUCTIVITY
Edward Deming (Consultant in Statistics)	Complexity in quality control. Overuse of computer printouts.	More statisticians on the plant floor.
Amitai Etzioni (Professor, George Washington University)	Oil price hikes. Obsolescence of capital.	Profit-sharing plans. Termination of support to sick industries.
Miltion Friedman (Senior Research Fellow, Hoover Institute)	High marginal tax rates. Inflation. Excessive governmental regulation.	Taming of inflation. Reduction of the role of the government.
Herman Kahn (Director of Research, Hudson Institute)	Hedonism of middle class.	Termination of support to sick industries. Subsidization of computers, telecommunications, data processing.
Robert Kurtz (Senior Vice President, President,General Electric)	A whole array	Good work manaagement. Robots.
Lloyd McBride (International President, United Steelworks of American)	Adversarial relationship of management and workers.	Collective bargaining.
William Miller (Vice President, U.S. Steel)	International competition.	Plant floor collaboration, but not management-worker committees.
Paul Samuelson (Institute Professor, M.I.T.)	Oil price hikes. World recession. Inflation. Disincentives to save, such as Social Security.	Capital formation. Knowledge accumulation.
Lester Thurow (Professor, M.I.T.)	A whole array internally. International competition	Subsidization of "sunrise" industries. Retraining of work force of "sick" industries.
Gordon Wallis (Chief Executive Officer, Irving Trust)	Inflation. Reduction in capital formation.	Reduction in Government spending. Change of attitudes towards success.

Note: Names in Alphabetical Order

association of symptoms with causes and appropriate remedies for the identified problems.

To this end, we will attempt, as a first step, to develop a productivity measure that we feel is theoretically satisfying, statistically efficient, and technically feasible to generate at the firm level. It is at this level that managerial decisions must be appropriately motivated. Furthermore, this measure must be amenable to aggregation, so that the information it provides is useful for the industry and may also serve as an input to public policy decisions associated with the industry.

We start in this paper by reviewing the existing literature in order to identify the theoretical underpinnings of productivity analysis, and determine the approaches or methodologies that have been utilized by researchers in the field. We then develop two theoretical models which aid in a synthesis and discussion of most of the relevant concepts gleaned from the literature, and which we will use later on to derive criteria for testing the effectiveness of productivity measures.[2] Finally, we develop our conclusions from this discussion.

---

[2]This will be the topic of another paper where we will set certain criteria against which we will test the statistical properties of alternative productivity measures. We will also apply some of these measures to two firms in the automobile industry.

II. MAJOR APPROACHES: A LITERATURE REVIEW

A. Basic Approaches

Our literature review revealed the following four basic approaches to productivity analysis: production function, econometric, growth accounting, and behavioral science.[3]

Those researchers using the production function approach assume that the growth of output can be attributed to input growth and technological progress. To identify the contribution of these input factors, a translog production function with constant returns to scale is generally assumed, capturing most of the characteristics of a twice-differentiable production function.[4] In translog functions, the outputs are exponential functions of the logarithm of inputs. Accordingly, productivity growth is defined as the difference between the growth rate of output and that of inputs. Techniques such as econometrics are used in estimating the translog functions from which productivity growth is then derived (See Appendix 1 for more details).

In contrast, those using the pure econometric aoproach do not restrict themselves to the factors focused on in the production function approach. They believe that other factors may make significant contributions to productivity growth, such as R&D expenditures and technology. They employ econometric models where the dependent variable is productivity and the independent variables are factors believed to affect it. By examining the statistical significane of the coefficients of the independent variables, hypothesized relationships can be confirmed--although causality cannot necessarily be so established.

---

[3]These are neither mutually exclusive nor independent classifications. They are only used for expositional purposes.

The third approach, growth accounting, assumes a competitive market where the earnings of each factor of production equal the value of its product when fully employed. The contributions of inputs are measured by their market return. Output growth may then be attributed to labor and capital by weighting the growth in hours worked and the expansion of the capital stocks by their respective gains (See Appendix 2).

The final approach is what we categorize as behavioral science. In contrast to the other approaches, the unit of analysis here is more at the firm level and even to that of the individual. Instead of focusing on structured or economic factors, behavioral science pays attention to a variety of firm-specific and individual-specific variables such as motivation, organizational structure, and the like. The methodologies used under this approach vary considerably, but often will include questionnaires, surveys, interviews, and observations. While much of the data are 'soft', this approach often provides pertinent information or insights regarding the behavior of those who make decisions that are not found in the others.[5]

B. Major Contributions

The work on productivity is voluminous, so we have selected for presentation what we believe are the major theoretical contributions to the understanding of productivity and its measurement, and/or are representatives of the four major approaches, i.e. production function, econometric, growth accounting, and behavioral science, described above.The quoted works are listed alphabetically by author.

---

[5]Researchers favoring the behavioral science approach to productivity reflect in their work the influence of people such as: Barnard (1938), Roethlisberger and Dickson (1939), Simon (1945), Maslow (1954), March and Simon (1958), MacGregor (1960), March (1963), Woodward (1965), and Thompson (1967) to mention a few.

1. Edward Denison's <u>Accounting for United States Economic Growth: 1929-1969</u> (1974) is a seminal work utilizing the growth accounting approach Denison's intellectual approach is very useful, in that it delineates measurement problems and methodologies related to input and output. The author develops numerous indices for various components of input and output and then combines them for an overall index of output over input.

   For input he examines labor, land, and capital. The components of labor input that he uses are: a) employment, b) average and total hours-worked, c) age-sex composition, and d) education of workers. Land is a singular variable, and business capital consists of inventories, structures and equipment.

   Denison uses national income as output and thus, combining with the inputs above, arrives at an output per unit of input figure. He then examines the effects of different 'irregular factors' on this measure such as: a) gains from reallocation of resources, b) changes in utilization intensity of employed resources resulting from work stoppages and fluctuation in demand intensity, c) economies of scale, and d) advances in knowledge.

2. Denison's "Explanation of Declining Productivity Growth" (1979) is a later work by the same author as above, dealing with U.S. growth in the 1970's. In it, he discusses a number of commonly offered reasons for productivity decline.

   In the area of advances in knowledge, he stresses the adverse impact of curtailment of R & D, the decline in opportunities for major advances, the decline in U.S. ingenuity, and the increased lag in the appreciation of knowledge due to the aging of capital. Other potential causes of productivity decline, according to Denison, are the effects of government regulation and excessive taxation, misallocation of resources, dilution of executive attention, delay of new projects, disincentives for savings and efficiency by inflation, the lessening of competitive pressure, changes in the quality of management, the rise in energy prices, and a shift of high-quality resources (especially manpower) from manufacturing to services. The author presents a thorough discussion of these factors but is unable to draw firm conclusions or to quantify their effects on productivity.

3. Barbara M. Fraumeni and Dale W. Jorgensen, in a paper entitled "Capital Formation and U.S. Productivity Growth, 1948-1976" (1981), utilize the production function approach examining the relationship between capital formation and productivity growth. For each of forty-six industries, they took industry output to be a translog function of the capital, labor and intermediate inputs.[6] The growth of output, holding all inputs constant, is defined to be a rate of technical change or productivity growth.

They derived the rate of technical change to be the logarithmic difference between aggregate output and weighted inputs, from one period to another, where the weight of each input is the average ratio of the input to output value.[7]

---

[6]Specifically, they characterize it as follows:

$$V_t = (\ln Z_t - \ln Z_{t-1}) - V_x (\ln X_t - \ln X_{t-1}) - V_k(\ln K_t - \ln K_{t-1})$$
$$- V_\ell(\ell n L_t - \ell n L_{t-1})$$

Where V_t is the rate of technical change; Z_t is the output at time t; X_t is the intermediate input at time t; K_t is the capital input at time t; L_t is the labor input at time t.

V_x, V_k, V_ℓ are given by: $V_x = 1/2(V_{x,t} + V_{x,t-1})$; $V_K = 1/2(V_{k,t} + V_{k,t-1})$

and $V_\ell = 1/2(V_{\ell,t} + V_{\ell,t-1})$; where $V_{x,t} = (P_x \cdot X)/(P_t \cdot Z_t)$;

$V_{K,t} = (P_K \cdot K)/(P_t \cdot Z_t)$; and $V_{\ell,t} = (P_\ell \cdot L)/(P_t \cdot Z_t)$.

[7]This holds true based on the characteristics of the translog function and on an equilbrium condition where the share of each input in terms of value of output is equal to the elasticity of output with respect to these inputs.

Their finding was that the rate of technical change disappeared as a source of economic growth after 1966. They also conclude that the contribution of capital input is the most important source of growth in aggregate value added.

They assume that the capital input of an industry is a translog function which is the accumulation of past investments less efficiency loss (replacement rate). Therefore, estimates of capital stock require data on both investments and replacement rate. They first compile data on investment for each industry for the period 1948-1976 by four legal forms of organization (corporate business, non-corporate business, private households, and non-profit institutions) and by six asset types (producers' durable equipment, consumers' durables, tenant-occupied residential structures, owner-occupied residential structures, inventories, and land), which are the components of capital stock.

Concerning efficiency loss, they assume that 1) the efficiency of capital goods in the form of equipment and structures declines geometrically with the age of the asset and 2) there is no efficiency loss in both land and inventories. To determine the rate of decline in efficiency of an asset they use the double declining balance depreciation method. (Such that if n is the lifetime of the asset, the replacement rate, δ, is estimated to be 2/n).

Estimates of capital stock were thus obtained by summing past investments less efficiency loss. Namely, A_t^i, the stock of asset i at time t, is:

$$A_t^i = \sum_{\tau=0}^{t} = (1-\delta)^{\tau} I^i{}_{t-\tau}$$

Where δ is the replacement rate and $I^i_{t-\tau}$ is the investment in asset i at time $t-\tau$.

The capital input, then, is expressed as a weighted translog function of these components of the capital stock.

4. Frank M. Gollop and Dale W. Jorgenson in "U.S. Productivity Growth by Industry, 1947-1973" (1980) continue the production function work, here assuming constant returns to scale and using data from various published sources to estimate the necessary parameters.

The authors disaggregate the labor input of all employed persons into categories cross-classified by sex, eight age groups, and fifty-one industries. They then assign total labor hous along each row and columnof their multiproportional matrix and calculate the actual hours worked by each group of workers. The purpose of the mutliproportional matrix model is to estimate the elements of matrix B whose row and column sums are known from a known matrix A, by assuming the elements in B are proportional to the elements of A. The same technique is employed for labor compensation deriving the actual compensation per job. The product of actual hours worked times actual compensation thus gives the value-added of input (including transportation costs and all taxes on primary and intermediate inputs).

Capital stock, land, and inventory are considered as capital inputs. Capital stock is not adjusted for its utilization rate, but is adjusted for replacement rate, technological change, and land appreciation (See Appendix 3 for more on the multiproportional matrix).

Finally, value added in constant constant dollars is used as the measure of output (net of indirect business taxes, sales and excise taxes, and trade and transportation margins associated with delivery of the output). Their work is significant in the voluminous amount of data amassed and analyzed on an industry by industry basis, noting the changes in productivity for each industry.

5. J. T. Hall and R. A. Dixon in Productivity Measurement in R & D (1975) focus on measurement of a specific business function, but it is instructive as an illustration of the behavioral science approach, in this case studying the work process through interviews and work samples. They define dimensions of productivity as follows:

Phase	Measurement Factor
Inputs	Value of Input
Process	Efficiency
Output	Value of Output: Volume, Quality, Utility (Impact)

They state that input and efficiency are relatively quantifiable but output is more elusive, particularly because it should be measured, they contend, in terms of individual, organizational, and societal goals. In attempting to measure output they utilize a technique called 'value analysis' which basically involves developing criteria for benefits, with assigned weights, thus obtaining an overall output measure. Another method they propose is a survey of users of technology as to the impact of R & D output.

6. S.A. Horwitz and A. Sherman's "A Direct Measure of the Relationship Between Capital and Productivity" (1980) is another example of the behavioral science approach. They attempt to obtain direct estimates of relationships between characteristics reflecting human capital and the productivity of workers in industrial occupations.

Among their findings are that: a) the productivity of enlisted men (Navy) was a function of their characteristics and training, b) those in higher pay grades and those having more experinece were more productive, c) the entry test scores often predict performance, and d) training enhances productivity.

7. Richard Kopcke's "Potential Growth, Productivity and Capital Accumulation" (1980) is in the econometrics tradition. He argues that value-added is the proper measure of output because it avoids double-counting. He further argues that accounting identities require that factor products must equal factor income, i.e. GNP = compensation of labor, plus return to capital, plus the earnings of renters (before taxes). However, while this holds true as a theoretical identity, reality may differ from the ideal.

Another contention of the author is that energy is not a factor of production: it is a produced material input and its price can influence the growth of potential output and productivity because it can:

a) Influence the choice of production techniques

b) Encourage/discourage technical innovation, and

c) Change relative costs of factors of production

8. Edwin Mansfield's "Basic Research and Productivity Increases in Manufacturing" (1980) is another econometric approach. This author assumes value added to be a function of capital, labor, the industry's stock of both basic and applied research, and an exponential coefficient of growth. He ran regression analyses of total factor productivity against four ratios: a) applied research expenditure to value added; b) basic research expenditure to value added; c) the percent of the industry's workers that are union members; and d) percent of R&D expenditure that is embodied in an industry's purchased inputs.

His findings were that all of the above ratios were significant in predicting productivity. Mansfield also uses firm data to test the robustness of the above model and obtains similar results.

9. J. Norsworthy, M. Harper, and K. Kunze in "The Slowdown in Productivity Growth: Analysis of some Contributing Factors" (1979) make the empirical observation that labor productivity in the private business sector grew 1% per year from 1973 to 1978, about one third of the growth rate realized from 1948 to 1965.

In their analysis Norsworthy et. al assume a purely competitive market and employ a translog production funtion. They adjusted both labor input and capital input for changes in quality caused by changes in compensation and inter-sectoral shifts. Further adjustments were made to labor inputs for hours worked vs. hours paid and to capital inputs for allocations to pollution abatement equipment. They did not adjust for technological improvement.

Contrary to what some researchers in the area of productivity have hypothesized, these authors found complementarity between energy and capital in the U.S. rather than substitution of one for the other. They also examined the substitution of labor and capital. They found for the period 1965 to 1973 that both energy and capital prices went up,[8] yet the price of labor grew faster than the price of capital by 4%. Thus the capital was more attractive than labor. However, from 1973 to 1978 the price of labor was growing faster than the price of capital at

---

[8]The price of capital is calculated through the present value method. Namely, the price of capital is the discount rate which equals the present value of both the cash flows and the purchase price of capital.

a rate of 1%. During this latter period there was a marked drop in capital formation as labor was used to replace capital, in terms of costs of inputs as measured.

10. George L. Perry's "Potential Output and Productivity" (1977) is unique in that it deals with potential versus actual quantities and projects future productivity changes. Perry uses econometric methods to estimate labor-force participation in the work force based on unemployment data from the Bureau of Labor Statistics. The labor force is also adjusted for age and sex composition based on demographic data. Using such data he derives a potential labor input figure and then calculates the potential output. In his calculations Perry uses quantities rather than wages or prices and assumes an optimistic growth in GNP for his potential output calculation. Then certain functional forms are utilized (e.g. exponentials) as are empirical laws (Okun's laws) in order to compare potential versus actual output/input. He uses several equations relating output and unemployment rates and compares their coefficients with Okun's law coefficient.[9] The unexplained residuals in his regression analysis are then attributed to productivity increases/decreases. Based on his results, the author projected that productivity would increase after 1977.

11. R. C. Scheppach, Jr. and L. C. Woehlcke's Transportation Productivity (1975) is a study which examines various measures of output and inputs. They suggest that output should be measured as the net of intermediate inputs, with adjustements for price and quality changes. Capital input should be measured in constant dollars and adjusted for

---

[9]Okun's law says that for every three percentage points growth in real GNP above the trend rate, the unemployment rate declines by one

the heterogeneity of the capital stocks by weighting the capital stocks by their respective rental prices. Finally, labor input should be measured as total worker's hours worked, adjusted for quality by considering the age and sex composition, level of education, and occupation of the workers.

III. THEORETICAL MODELS

From the previous discussion we can see that researchers have used a great number of measures in order to estimate both the level of productivity and its rate of change over time. What we need now is a framework which can be used to organize and facilitate our discussion of the relevant concepts related to productivity measurement. Some of these concepts are reflected in the work of the aforementioned researchers, and the rest, we feel, should have been encompassed. There are many ways to approach this task, but after reflection, we have decided to develop and analyze two different theoretical models in order to provide the enabling framework for discussion.

A. Definitions and Assumptions

Before we present the models, it is necessary that we provide some preliminary definitions and assumptions. Specifically, we need to define the particular properties of the production and cost functions involved. For a profit maximizing firm or industry, we can represent the producition process as follows:

$$\left\{\begin{matrix}\text{Total}\\\text{Input}\end{matrix}\right\} \longrightarrow \boxed{\text{Production Process}} \longrightarrow \left\{\begin{matrix}\text{Total}\\\text{Output}\end{matrix}\right\}$$

or

$$\{X\} \longrightarrow F(X,Y) \longrightarrow \{Y\}$$

or

$$\left\{\begin{matrix}X_1\\X_2\\.\\.\\.\end{matrix}\right\} \longrightarrow \begin{matrix}F(X_1,\ldots X_m\ ,\ Y_1\ldots,Y_n)\\(m\ \text{times}\ n)\end{matrix} \longrightarrow \left\{\begin{matrix}Y_1\\Y_2\\.\\.\\.\end{matrix}\right\}$$

where F(.) is a regular, monotonic, and convex function.

Applying the concept of duality mapping we can alternatively have:

{Cost of Inputs} ⟶ [Cost Function] ⟶ {Value of Outputs}

or

$$\{W^{-1}\}\cdot\{X\} \longrightarrow C(W,Y) \longrightarrow \{P^{-1}\}\cdot\{Y\}$$

or

$$\{W_1\ W_2 \ldots W_m\} \cdot \begin{Bmatrix} X_1 \\ X_2 \\ \cdot \\ \cdot \\ \cdot \\ X_m \end{Bmatrix} \rightarrow \underset{(m \text{ times } n)}{C(W_1 \ldots W_m, Y_1, \ldots Y_n)} \rightarrow \{P_1\ P_2 \ldots P_n\} \cdot \begin{Bmatrix} Y_1 \\ Y_2 \\ \cdot \\ \cdot \\ \cdot \\ Y_n \end{Bmatrix}$$

where W and P may be functions of time, and the cost function C(.) is nondecreasing, homogeneous of degree one, concave, and continuous in W. Admittedly, this specification is quite simplified -- and some may argue, unrealistic -- but it is useful for our purposes here as a point of departure to launch our discussion.

B. <u>Model 1: Production Function Approach</u>

The production function approach looks at productivity in terms of technical efficiency. Thus, the rate of change of productivity is defined as the precentage change of the output-input ratio over time (irrespective of physical units or dollars) i.e.

$$\%\Delta \text{ Productivity} = \%\Delta \left(\frac{\text{outputs } Y}{\text{inputs } X}\right) \tag{1}$$

If one accepts (1) above as a legitimate way to approach the subject of productivity change, the next issue is whether one should focus on all inputs or on a single input (such as labor, for example).

1. The case of all factor inputs. Assuming that output is a function of the inputs X (which in turn change over time), we can define total factor productivity as follows:[10]

$$TFP = \frac{(Y/X)_{t+1} - (Y/X)_t}{(Y/X)_t} \qquad (2)$$

Where Y and X represent all output and input factors respectively.If we look at this in a finite moment of time we arrive at the following:

$$TFP = \frac{Y^{t+1} - Y^t}{Y^t} - \frac{X^{t+1} - X^t}{X^t} \qquad (3)$$

This says that total factor productivity is approximately equal to the difference between the percentage change in total ouput and the percentage change in total inputs. If only one output and/or input are involved in the technological process under study, then it would be trivial to construct a time-series based on (3) and then extimate TFP. However, it is when more than one output and/or input are involved that one output and/or input are involved that a critical issue faces

---

[10]Stated in calculus form,

$$TFP = \frac{d}{dt}\ (\frac{Y}{X})/(Y/X) \ = \ (X\frac{dY}{dt} - Y\frac{dx}{dt})/(X^2 \ . \ (Y/X))$$

or

$$TFP = (\frac{dY}{dt})/Y - (\frac{dX}{dt})/X$$

researchers as to how to weight the output and/or inputs in order to calculate, in a meaningful way, total output and total input. Theoretically, these weights can be derived from either the production function or from its dual, the cost function. The question arises, however, as to whether these weights should be constant or should change over time. Researchers who use constant weights derived from a production function implicitly assume that the latter is piecewise linear. Otherwise, weights cannot be constant but should be functions of the level of inputs, a condition which presumes detailed knowledge of the functional form and the coefficients of the production function.

If the detailed knowledge as described above is not available, which is generally the case, one may derive approximate weights for inputs and outputs by using value added or revenues for outputs, and costs for inputs. However, in our opinion, to use the share of revenue of an output as a weight is conceptually incorrect because a product may claim a high share of revenue and, as a result, indicate high productivity, while, in fact, very little output may have been contributed per level of inputs, when intermediate inputs are subtracted.[11]

The use and careful calculation of value added would eliminate the problems associated with the use of revenue. We will, therefore, continue to build this model by utilizing a weighting scheme where outputs are weighted by their share of value added and inputs by their share of costs. In notation

---

[11]A good example of this is oil products. While high prices mean high revenue share, once the price of crude is subtracted, little contribution to output is exhibited. This also demonstrates that the choice of factors of production is very critical.

form we can write:

Value added share

for output $i = v_i = V_i/V$ and

Cost share for

input $j = w_j = W_j/W$

We can then rewrite equation (3) and add weights for all m inputs and n outputs:

$$TFP = \sum_{i=1}^{n} v_i^t \frac{Y_i^{t+1}}{Y_i^t} - \sum_{j=1}^{m} w_j^t \frac{X_j^{t+1}}{X_j^t} \tag{4}$$

where, of course, the sum of each set of weights

$(\sum_{i=1}^{n} v_i, \sum_{j=1}^{m} w_j)$ equals 1.

Equation (4) then accounts for all changes, over time, in the difference between outputs and inputs weighted in terms of their respective value added and costs. We are still concerned with the measurement of technical efficiency but put in terms that are more available and meaningful.

2. The case of one input. We now examine the other case previously mentioned, that is, where only one input factor is utilized in measuring productivity. As far as methodology is concerned, the derivation of single factor productivity (SFP) is the same as with TFP but there is no need for weighting of the input factor in this case. Thus, we can define the Single Factor Productivity as

$$SFP = \%\Delta \frac{\text{OUTPUT } Y}{\text{INPUT } X_j} \tag{5}$$

or, as before,

$$SFP = \frac{Y^{t+1} - Y^{t}}{Y^{t}} \quad \frac{X_j^{t+1} - X_j^{t}}{X_j^{t}} \tag{6}$$

Employing weights for outputs Y, we get

$$SFP = \left(\sum_{i=1}^{n} v_i^t \frac{Y_i^{t+1}}{Y_i^{t}} \right) - \frac{X_j^{t+1}}{X_j^{t}} \tag{7}$$

Comparing equations (4) and (7) we can see that there is apparently little difference between measures of SFP and TFP. Both do provide some measure of the relative technical efficiency of the production process. It is also obvious that the SFP measure would be easier to calculate because it requires fewer data as well as less manipulation. However, while this simplicity may be empirically facilitating, there is a loss that is suffered that needs to be acknowledged, though perhaps it is obvious, in that the signals it provides to managers, industry analysts, and government policy makers are not as rich and complete as the Total Factor Productivity measure. While labor productivity, for example, is extremely important, it is also vital to know what is the change in the productivity of other input factors as well, and also the possible interrelationships between them. A good case in point is the fact that while most of the productivity studies use measures similar to Equation (6), (with X_j being labor), they are unable to explain a large portion of productivity change.[12]

---

[12]For example, see Denison (1974)

Therefore, it might be useful to extend our model one step further, and focus on the unexplained or residual part of the total factor productivity (UTFP), defined as:

$$UTFP = TFP - SFP$$

Substituting (4) and (7) in the above we get:

$$UTFP = \frac{X_j^{t+1}}{X_j^t} - \sum_{j=1}^{m} w_j^t \frac{X_j^{t+1}}{X_j^t} \qquad (8)$$

Relation (8) points out a gap in productivity measures that must be identified and understood, and an area where we hope to make some progress as our work proceeds.

C. Model 2: Value Added Approach

While our first model focused on technical efficiency, this model looks at productivity in terms of economic efficiency, which is defined as the percentage rate of change over time in the ratio of output value added over input factor costs, i.e.

$$\Delta \text{ Productivity} = \% \, \Delta \; \frac{\text{Value Added of Outputs } Y}{\text{Cost of Inputs } X}$$

As with Model 1, we can again differentiate between total and single factor productivity. In examining the former, we can define TFP as follows:

$$TFP = \frac{\frac{d}{dt}\left(\frac{\sum_{i=1}^{n} V_i Y_i}{\sum_{j=1}^{m} W_j X_j}\right)}{\frac{\sum_{i=1}^{n} V_i Y_i}{\sum_{j=1}^{m} W_j X_j}} \qquad \text{For n outputs and m inputs} \qquad (9)$$

where all notations is the same as in Model 1. V_i, value added per unit of product i, can be defined as:

$$V_i = \frac{P_i}{\eta_i} - \frac{\sum_{j=1}^{L} w_j^i x_j^i}{Y_i} \qquad (10)$$

where P_i = market price of product i,

η_i = market power factor for product i,

w_j^i, x_j^i = cost, quantity of input raw material j going to product i, and

L = m less the primary input factors, which in our case are capital and labor, i.e. $L = m - 2$.

Equation (10) says that the value added of a particular product is the difference between the price of the product and the unit cost of intermediate inputs for that product. Note, however, that we have adjusted the market price by dividing by the market power factor η. This is because, ideally, we would like to know "real" productivity, i.e. where the market price reflects the true value of the product and does not reflect market power as well. Price for the pure monopoly is theoretically determined by the formula:

$$P = MC/[1 - (1/|E|)]$$

where MC represents marginal cost and E the elasticity of demand. In a purely competitive market, the elasticity is presumed to be infinite, and thus P = MC. In a pure natural monopoly this E may be close to zero. In the same manner, other market structures (oligopoly, imperfect competition) would show a deviation from the purely competitive price. Of course, η is difficult if not impossible to measure in the real world, and thus, the market price is generally used without any adjustment. We do feel, however, that the presence of market power as compounding factor needs to be explicitly understood and accounted for -- if not quantitatively, at least qualitatively.

Now, with equation (9) we can perform further manipulations and arrive at a much more disaggregated derivation of Total Factor Productivity:[13]

$$TFP = \frac{\sum_{i=1}^{n} \frac{\dot{P}_i Y_i}{\eta_i}}{A - B} + \frac{\sum_{i=1}^{n} \frac{P_i \dot{Y}_i}{\eta_i}}{A - B} - \frac{\sum_{i=1}^{n} \frac{P_i Y_i \dot{\eta}_i}{\eta_i^2}}{A - B} - \frac{\sum_{i=1}^{n} \sum_{j=1}^{L} w_j^i x_j^i}{A - B}$$

$$- \frac{\sum_{i=1}^{n} \sum_{j=1}^{L} w_j^i x_j^i}{A - B} - \frac{\sum_{j=1}^{m} \dot{W}_j X_j}{C} - \frac{\sum_{j=1}^{m} W_j^i \dot{X}_j^i}{C} \qquad (11)$$

Where $A = \sum_{i=1}^{n} \frac{P_i Y_i}{\eta_i}$ (Total Output Revenue, adjusted for market power)

$B = \sum_{i=1}^{n} \sum_{i=1}^{L} w_j^i x_j^i$ (Total Input Costs, excluding capital and labor)

$C = \sum_{j=1}^{m} W_j X_j$ (Total Input Costs, including capital and labor

[13]See Appendix 4 for the derivation.

(The dot over a variable indicates the representation of a relative change over time, e.g.[14]

$$P_t = \frac{P_t - P_{t-1}}{P_{t-1}}$$

This may appear somewhat foreboding, but if we examine each term in the equation, we can isolate the various components of productivity. We present each of the terms in Table 2. We can observe that each term has a primary variable that changes over time while all others remain constant. We also provide in the Table an example of activities or situations that may bring about a change in the primary factor in that term and also the directional effect of such a change on productivity.

[14] In a similar manner as before, we can also derive a SFP index w.r.t. the kth input factor such that

$$SFP_k = \frac{\frac{d}{dt}\frac{\sum_{i=1}^{n} V_i Y_i}{W_k X_k}}{\frac{\sum_{i=1}^{n} V_i Y_i}{W_k X_k}}$$

The end result is the same as equation (11) with the exception of the last two terms which would be:

$$\frac{\dot{W}_k X_k}{W_{\cdot} X_{\cdot}} \text{ and } \frac{W_k X_k}{W_{\cdot} X_{\cdot}}$$

NO.	EQUATION TERM	PRIMARY VARIABLE	EFFECT ON TFP OF CHANGE IN PRIMARY VARIABLE	EXAMPLE OF SITUATION WHICH MAY CAUSE CHANGE IN PRIMARY VARIABLE
11a	$\frac{\sum_{i=1}^{n} \frac{P_i Y_i}{\eta_i}}{A - B}$	P_i Market Price	+	Exploitation of market opportunity; market segmentation, product differentiation using price as a strategic dimension.
11b	$\frac{\sum_{i=1}^{n} \frac{P_i \dot{Y}_i}{\eta_i}}{A - B}$	Y_i Output Quanity	+	Increase in output through technical/ technological change and/or capital/labor ratio; same workers produce more; Capital more productive.
11c	$\frac{\sum_{i=1}^{n} \frac{P_i \dot{Y}_i h}{\eta_i^2}}{A - B}$	η_i Market Power Factor	-	Monopoly advantage and market elasticity not reflected in the market price.
11d	$\frac{\sum_{i=1}^{n} \sum_{j=1}^{L} \dot{W}_j^i X_j^i}{A - B}$	W_j^i Input Price (1) (excluding capital and labor)	-	OPEC decision on oil prices causes raw materials' prices to increase.
11e	$\frac{\sum_{i=1}^{n} \sum_{j=1}^{L} W_j^i \dot{X}_j^i}{A - B}$	X_j^i Input Quantity (1) (excluding capital and labor)	-	Less pure ore might require more raw materials for same level of output production.
11f	$\frac{\sum_{j=1}^{m} \dot{W}_j X_j}{C}$	W_j Input Price (2) (including capital and labor)	-	Wages increase; interest rates rise, causing increase in cost of capital.
11g	$\frac{\sum_{j=1}^{m} W_j \dot{X}_j}{C}$	X_j Input Quantity (2) (including capital and labor)	-	More labor required for same level of output production.

The first three terms (11a - 12c) reflect changes in output i.e. in the numerator of the productivity measure, while thelast four (11d - 11g) deal with changes in input i.e. in the denominator.

The first term identifies the effect a change in market price will have on productivity. Ceteris paribus, an increase in the price will indicate an increase in productivity. Such a situation might occur, for example, when market segments allow firms to raise prices in a segment, whether that segmentation occurs due to geographical limitations or product characteristics.

Term 11b represents the effect of a change in output quantity while the amount of input remains unchanged. This might be due to technological change which allows for more effective use of labor and/or capital. An increase would naturally reflect an increase in productivity.

The third component measures the effect of a change in market power, which is negatively correlated with productivity. As noted, a situation where this might occur is where some monopoly advantage exists, which is not reflected in the market price.

If we look at the terms dealing with input changes (11d - 11g), we see basically the effect of changes in either quantities or prices. Of course, any increase would increase the denominator and, thus, decrease productivity, if all other things remain constant.

The first two of these look at changes in inputs other than capital and labor. Both an input price increase for crude oil, for example, as generated by OPEC pricing decisions, or a declining mineral deposit with less pure ore being mined causing more inputs to be utilized, both would cause a decrease in productivity.

The last two terms also reflect similar situations and effects, but these input changes include changes in capital and/or labor. As indicated, examples might be a change in wages dictated by union contracts or COLA, or a slowdown in the amount of work contributed by workers. Both situations would cause productivity to decline, again if all other things remain constant.

This disaggregation may also help us to understand what are the controllable and non-controllable variables in productivity. It is, of course, useful to decision-makers to know about changes in variables over which they have no control, but it is much more useful to know the effect of those over which one has control.

Unfortunately, this is not an entirely clear-cut matter. We can say, generaly speaking, that some variables are primarily external to the firm, i.e. they are generally considered as "givens". This might include market price (exclusive of market power). We can also fairly confidently assert that all of the factors place some limits or bounds on firm's initiative. However, it also seems plausible that the firm can exercise a certain amount of control over many of the factors -- and that this may differ among firms in an industry -- or across industries. One example is input prices. While to a large extent the firm has little control over these prices, market structure may allow certain larger firms to extract concessions from suppliers in terms of prices (See Porter, 1980). While it is not our purpose here to elaborate on this point, we must nonetheless keep it in mind.

D. A Comparison

As a final aspect of our analysis, we reproduct the comments of professionals provided earlier in Table 1, but now relating them to our framework from equation (11).

Table 3 offers a valuable insight with respect to the complexity of the productivity problem because it clearly shows two facts. First, each expert has focused on a limited number of the variables explaing the productivity problem as posited by our theoretical models. Second, each expert has focused on a different set of variables.

More specifically, we attempt in Table 3 to classify the major causes of productivity decline in recent years according to the framework developed in our theoretical models. Although some of the variables are not quantifiable, we venture to account for the quantifiable ones. There is of course a much deeper analysis behind the opinions expressed by these professionals, in the form of empirical research or accumulated experience. For our expository purposes we will satisfy ourselves with the demonstration that no one has really covered the whole spectrum of causes, and that the set of variables potentially accounted in their ceteris paribus argument is different for each one of them.

E. Deming sees complexity in quality control and blind faith in computers as major causes of productivity decline. Our framework can account and empirically test this conculsion by measuring the impact of change in quantities of inputs classified by quality, on productivity ceteris paribus. Based on our theoretical model we expect negative correlation.

A. Etzioni sees oil price hikes and obsolescence of capital as major causes of productivity decline. Our framework can account and empirically test this conclusion by measuring the impact of changes in prices and quantities of inputs and quantity, classified by quality, of output on producivity ceteris paribus. Based on our theoretical model we expect the correlation to be negative with respect to inputs and positive with respect to output.

M. Friedman sees high marginal tax rates, inflation and excessive governmental regulation as major causes of productivity decline. Our framework cannot account for macroeconomic effects such as tax changes but can account and empirically test his other conclusitions by measuring the impact of changes in price of output, input, and quantity of input mandated by regulation (e.g. pollution abatement equipment) on productivity ceteris

	CAUSES OF PRODUCTIVITY DECLINE IN RECENT YEARS	RELEVANT VARIABLES FROM OUR FRAMEWORK
Edward Deming (Consultant in (lle, llg) Statistics)	Complexity in quality control. Overuse of computer printouts.	Input quantity
Amitai Etzioni (Professor, George Washington University)	Oil price hikes Obsolescence of capital.	Output quantity(llb) Input price (lld) Input quantity (llg)
Milton Friedman (Senior Research Fellow, Hoover Institute)	High marginal tax rates. Inflation. Excessive governmental regulation.	Non quantifiable Market price (lla, lld,llf) Input quantity (lle, llg)
Herman Kahn (Director of Research, Hudson Institute)	Hedonism of middle class.	Non quantifiable
Robert Kurtz (Senior Vice President, General Electric)	A whole array.	Non quantifiable
Lloyd McBride (International President, United Steelworkers of America)	Adversarial relationship of management and workers.	Input quantity (llg) Input price (llf)
William Miller (Vice President, U.S. Steel)	International competition.	Market price (lla) Market power factor (llc)
Paul Samnuelson (Institute Professor, M.I.T.)	Oil price hikes. World recession. Inflation. Disincentives to save, such as Social Security.	Input price (lla) Market price (lla) Market price (lla) Non quantifiable
Lester Thurow (Professor, M.I.T.)	A whole array internally. International competition.	Non quantifiable Market price (lla), Market power factor (llc)
Gordon Wallis (Chief Executive Officer, Irving Trust)	Inflation Reduction in capital formation.	Market price (lla) Input quantity (llg)

paribus. Based on our theoretical model we expect positive correlation with output price inflation and negative correlations with input price inflation and quantity increase.

H. Kahn sees hedonism of the middle class as a major cause of productivity decline. Our framework cannot account for such behavioral attributes, but only in an indirect sense, classifying labor by socioeconomic class.

R. Kurtz sees a great number of major causes of productivity decline, which is again beyond the capabilities of our model.

L. McBride sees the adversarial relationship of management and workers as the major cause of productivity decline. Our framework can account and empirically test this conclusion by measuring the impact of labor input, adjusted for days on strike and wage change, on productivity ceteris paribus. Based on our theoretical model we expect negative correlation.

W. Miller sees international competition as a major cause of productivity decline. Our framework can account and empirically test this conclusion by measuring the impact of price and market power changes on productivity ceteris paribus . Based on our theoretical model we expect negative correlation.

P. Samuelson sees oil price hikes, world recession, inflation and disincentives to save as major causes of productivity decline. Our framework cannot account for macroeconomic effects such as GNP growth and saving propensities, but can account for oil price hikes and inflation, as described above.

L. Thurow sees a great number of internal causes and international compeition as major causes of productivity decline. We have touched upon these causes above. Furthermore, Thurow introduces the concept of harvesting "sunset" industries and subsidizing "sunrise" industries. Our theoretical model can estimate elasticities of factors affecting productivity so that the most appropriate factors in an industry will be subsidized in order to increase productivity.

G. Wallis sees inflation and reduction in capital formation as major causes of productivity decline. We have presented our views with respect to these causes above.

IV. CONCLUSIONS

The problem of productivity definition and measurement has been in the forefront of economic research in the past few years. The importance of an increasing rate of change in productivity for an industry and for an economy as a whole is crucial, because it directly affects the prices of goods and the prices paid for labor and capital, and as a result, the rate of inflation.

Especially in a maturing industry or economy with a relatively competitive environemnt, increasing productivity is the only way to keep increasing real wages (i.e. wage over price) - and consequently the standard of living of the population. The future of the capitalistic economic system is very much dependent on how effectively this problem will be confronted.

The economic studies reviewed here reveal some aspects of the productivity decline puzzle. However, most of these studies take a macroeconomic point of view. They look from the level of industry up to that of the whole economy. This approach is theoretically and intuitively appealing, but very difficult to support empirically, and conclusions derived from such an approach are more appropriate for public policy decisions. Even for the latter, the support from the models is not causal-diagnostic, but symptomatic. Furthermore, the averaging process, which permits stability of behavior through aggregation, conceals, in our opinion, valuable information. That is why there is so much argument and such diversity of opinions as to what needs to be done at the macro-policy level.

Our approach, delineated in Table 2, looks from the industry level down to that of the firm, with the end objective of attempting to understand cause and effect relationships. This approach is both theoretically and intuitively acceptable, data are more readily available at this level, and conclusions reached are potentially more useful for managerial decisions. Furthermore, being close to the locus of decisons regarding technology and the allocation of resources, we may be able to understand better how decisions are made, what time lags are involved, and why some firms and industries are more successful than others.

In Table 2 we presented the quantifiable variables that affect the productivity growth rate and also the positive or negative effect that an increase of any one of the variables, other things being equal, is hypothesized to have on this growth rate. We do not, however, deal with the affect of a combination of variables on the rate of change. This is much more complex problem that is the subject of much ongoing research. We hope that sometime in the future we will be able to conduct field research on the signals provided to executives by alternative productivity measures and on the impact of the information generated on decisions regarding issues of productivity.

BIBLIOGRAPHY

1. Barnard, Chester, Functions of the Executive (Cambridge, MA: Harvard, 1938).

2. Cyert, Richard, and March, James, A Behavioral Theory of the Firm (Englewood Cliffs, N.J.: Prentice Hall, 1963).

3. Denison, E., Accounting for U.S. Economic Growth, 1929-1969 (Washington, D.C.: The Brookings Institution, 1974).

4. ________________, "Explanation of Declining U.S. Productivity Growth", Survey of Current Business (August, 1979, Part II), pp. 1-24.

5. Fraumeni, B., and Jorgenson, D., "Capital Formation and U.S. Productivity Growth, 1948-1976," in Productivity Analysis: A Range of Perspectives, ed., Ali Dogramaci (Boston: Martinus Nijhoff, 1981).

6. Gollop, F. M., and Jorgenson, D., "U.S. Productivity Growth by Industry, 1947-1973," in New Developments in Productivity Measurement and Analysis, ed., J. W. Kendrick and B. N. Vaccara (Chicago: University of Chicago Press, 1980), pp. 17-124.

7. Hall, J. T. and R. A. Dixon, Productivity Measurement in R&D, (Washington, D.C.: Government Printing Office, 1975).

8. Horowitz, S. A., and A. Sherman, "A Direct Measure of the Relationship Between Capital and Productivity," Journal of Human Resources (Winter, 1980), p. 67-76.

9. Kopcke, Richard, "Potential Growth, Productivity, and Capital Accumulation," New England Economic Review (May/June, 1980), pp. 22-41.

10 McGregor, D., The Human Side of Enterprise (New York: McGraw-Hill, 1960).

11. Mansfield, E., "Basic Research and Productivity Increase in Manufacturing," American Economic Review (December, 1980), pp. 863-873.

12. March, J., and H. A. Simon, Organizations (New York: Wiley, 1958).

13 Maslow, A., Motivation and Personality (New York: Harper and Brothers, 1954).

14. Norsworthy, J. R., Harper, M. J., and Kunze, K., "The Slowdown in Productivity Growth: Analysis of Some Contributing Factors" in Brookings Papers on Economic Activity, 1979: 2 (Washington, D.C.: The Brookings Institution, 1979), pp. 387-433.

15. Peat, Marwick, Mitchell & Co., World, Winter 1981 (New York: Peat, Marwick, Mitchell & Co., 1981).

16. Perry, George L., "Potential Output and Productivity" in Brookings Papers on Economic Activity, 1977: 1 (Washington, D.C.: The Brookings Institution, 1977), pp. 11-47.

17. Porter, Michael, Competitive Strategy (New York: Free Press, 1980).

18. Roethlisberger, F. J., and Dickson, W. J., Management and the Worker - An Account of a Research Program Conducted by Western Electric Co., Hawthorne Works, Chicago (Cambridge, MA: Harvard University Press, 1939).

19. Scheppach, R. C., Jr. and Woehlcke, L. C., Transportation Productivity (Lexington, MA: D. C. Heath and Co., 1975).

20. Simon, Herbert A., Administrative Behavior (New York: McGraw Hill, 1945).

21. Thompson, James D., Organizations in Action (New York: McGraw-Hill, 1967).

22. Woodward, J., Industrial Organization: Theory and Practice (London: Oxford University Press, 1965).

APPENDIX 1

AN EXPLANATION OF TRANSLOG PRODUCTION FUNCTION

A production function is a mathematical function that describes the relationship between inputs and outputs. Traditional production functions such as Constant Elasticities of Substitution and Cobb-Douglas have restrictions on their specifications. For example, McFadden (1963) has demonstrated that for more than one output or more than two input factors, CES production functions require highly restrictive conditions on the elasticity values. Translog production functions do not have restrictions on substitution and number of output or input factors. Besides they provide an approximation of any twice differentiable production function. For these reasons translog production functions have been more widely used in the past decade.

Translog production functions are quadratic in the logarithms of the quantities of inputs and outputs. For example, a translog production function of one output (Y) and three inputs, say capital (K), labor (L) and intermediate input (X) is:

$$\ell nY = \alpha_0 + \alpha_K \ell n\, K + \alpha_L \ell n\, L + \alpha_X \ell n\, X + \frac{1}{2} \beta_{KK}(\ell nK)^2 + \beta_{LL}(\ell nL)^2$$

$$+ \frac{1}{2} \beta_{XX}(\ell nX)^2 + \beta_{KL}\ \ell nK \cdot \ell n\, L + \beta_{KX}\ \ell nK + \beta_{LX}\ \ell nL \cdot \ell nX$$

APPENDIX 2

AN EXPLANATION OF THE GROWTH ACCOUNT METHOD

If we let y be the output and $X_1 \ldots X_n$ be n inputs, we can represent the production function as $y = f(X_1, X_2 \ldots X_n)$. The output growth, Δy, can then be obtained by differentiating the production function:

$$dy = \sum_{i=1}^{n} \frac{\partial f}{\partial X_i} dX_i \tag{1}$$

If all input factors are employed in competitive markets, the marginal product value of factor i (MPV_i) must be equal to its price. Thus, if we let

P_{x_i} be the price of factor x_i and P_y be the price of y, then,

$$MPV_i = \frac{\partial f}{\partial X} P_y = P_{x_i} \tag{2}$$

or rearranging

$$\frac{\partial f}{\partial X} = \frac{P_{x_i}}{P_y} \tag{3}$$

substituting (3) into (1) we have

$$dy = \sum_{i=1}^{n} \frac{P_{x_i}}{P_y} dX_i \tag{4}$$

Dividing both sides by and multiplying numerator and denominator of the right hand side by X_i

$$\frac{dy}{y} = \sum_{i=1}^{n} \frac{P_{x_i} \cdot X_i}{P_y \cdot Y} \frac{dX_i}{X_i} \qquad (5)$$

Equality (5) indicates that the growth rate of output $(\frac{dy}{y})$ is the sum of individual input factor growth rate$(\frac{dX_i}{x_i})$ times its share of the value of output $(\frac{P_{x_i} \cdot X_i}{P_y \cdot y})$. Thus, the contribution of an individual input factor to output growth is its share of the value of output times its own growth rate. A numerical example may clarify this. Suppose we have competitive markets for both outputs and inputs and capital and labor are the only two input factors. Assume the share of labor and capital to value added are 0.6 and 0.4 respectively and that labor increased, by 5%, and capital by 15%. Then, the contribution of labor to output is 3% (5% x .6) and that of capital is 6% (15% x 0.4). Now suppose that the above mentioned increases in inputs cause an increase of 12% in output. The residual of 3% which is the unexplained output growth (12% - 3% - 6%), may be attributed to technological change.

Of course one may question the applicability of the growth accounting method to the measurement of productivity in an economy where the markets are not perfectly competitive. While such skepticism has a general validity, to the extent that industries, and firms within an industry, are facing the same competitive conditions with respect to inputs and outputs the objections to growth accounting are instigated as regards interindustry and interfirm comparisions of productivity. This is especially true, if the comparisons are limited to ordinal rather than cardinal measures.

APPENDIX 3

THE MULTIPROPORTIONAL MATRIX MODEL

Jorgensen and Gollop have used the multiproportional matrix model to estimate hours worked and labor compensation per hour, cross-classified by sex, age, education, employment class, occupation, and industry. In order to illustrate this model we will use a biproportional matrix model as an example.

Consider two nonnegative m by n matrices, A and B. The elements of the matrix A (A_{ij}), and the row and column sums of the matrix B (P_i and q_j) are known. The problem is to use a_{ij}, P_i, and q_j to estimate the unknown elements of matrix B(b_{ij}).

The biproportional model assumes that the matrix B is biproportional to the matrix A if

$$b_{ij} = r_i \cdot s_j \cdot a_{ij}$$

where r_i is a factor associated with the ith row of A and s_j is a factor associated with the jth column of A. The problem of estimating b_{ij} reduces to the problem of choosing r_i and s_j so that the row column sums are equal to the known row and column sums, P_i and q_j. These r_i's and s_j's can be obtained through an iterative process.

Similarly, the multiproportional matrix model assumes that b_{ij} is the product of a_{ij} and many proportional factors such as r_i and s_j, so that the problem becomes one of estimating these factors through the iterative process.

APPENDIX 4

$$TFP = \frac{\dfrac{d}{dt}\dfrac{\sum_{i=1}^{n} V_i Y_i}{\sum_{j=1}^{m} W_j X_j}}{\dfrac{\sum_{i=1}^{n} V_i Y_i}{\sum_{j=1}^{m} W_j X_j}}$$

$$= \frac{\left(\frac{d}{dt}\sum_{i=1}^{n} V_i Y_i\right) * \left(\sum_{j=1}^{m} W_j X_j\right) - \left(\sum_{i=1}^{n} V_i Y_i\right)\left(\frac{d}{dt}\sum_{j=1}^{m} W_j X_j\right)}{\left(\sum_{j=1}^{m} W_j X_j\right)^2}$$

$$* \quad \frac{\left(\sum_{j=1}^{m} W_j X_j\right)}{\sum_{i=1}^{n} V_i Y_i}$$

$$= \frac{\left(\frac{d}{dt}\left(\sum_{i=1}^{n} V_i Y_i\right)\right)}{\sum_{i=1}^{n} V_i Y_i} - \frac{\frac{d}{dt}\left(\sum_{j=1}^{m} W_j X_j\right)}{\sum_{j=1}^{m} W_j X_j}$$

Substituting for V_i from equation (10) we then get:

$$TFP = \frac{\frac{d}{dt} \sum_{i=1}^{n} \left(\frac{P_i}{\eta_i} - \frac{\sum_{j=1}^{L} W_j^i X_j^i}{Y_i}\right) Y_i}{\sum_{i=1}^{n} \left(\frac{P_i}{\eta_i} - \frac{\sum_{j=1}^{L} W_j^i X_j^i}{}\right) Y_i} - \frac{\frac{d}{dt}\left(\sum_{j=1}^{m} W_j X_j\right)}{\sum_{i=1}^{m} W_j X_j}$$

Multiplying through, this becomes:

$$TFP = \frac{\frac{d}{dt} \sum_{i=1}^{n} \left(\frac{P_i Y_i}{\eta_i} - \sum_{i=1}^{n} \sum_{j=1}^{L} W_j^i X_j^i\right)}{\sum_{i=1}^{n} \frac{P_i Y_i}{\eta_i} - \sum_{i=1}^{n} \sum_{j=1}^{L} W_j^i X_j^i} - \frac{\frac{d}{dt}\left(\sum_{j=1}^{m} W_j X_j\right)}{\sum_{j=1}^{m} W_j X_j}$$

Assuming no constants over time,

$$TFP = \frac{\sum_{i=1}^{n} \frac{\dot{P}_i Y_i \eta_i + P_i \dot{Y}_i \eta_i - P_i Y_i \dot{\eta}_i}{\eta_i^2} - \sum_{i=1}^{n} \sum_{j=1}^{L} \left(\dot{W}_j^i X_j^i + W_j^i \dot{X}_j^i\right)}{\sum_{i=1}^{n} \frac{P_i Y_i}{\eta_i} - \sum_{i=1}^{n} \sum_{j=1}^{L} W_j^i X_j^i}$$

$$- \frac{\sum_{j=1}^{m} \left(\dot{W}_j X_j + W_j \dot{X}_j\right)}{\sum_{j=1}^{m} W_j X_j}$$

Rearranging, this becomes equation (11) as seen in the text.

Printed in Dunstable, United Kingdom

91223998R00027